LIGATURES

for black bodies

Denise Miller

Rattle | *Studio City, California* | 2016

Layout and design by Timothy Green

Cover art by Bridget A. Saunders
www.bas-photo.com

ISBN: 978-1-931307-32-1

First edition

The Rattle Foundation
12411 Ventura Blvd
Studio City, CA 91604
www.rattle.com

Contents

ACKNOWLEDGMENTS

Thank you to the editors of the journals and anthologies in which the following poems first appeared (sometimes in earlier versions):

Don't Erase Us (Rogue Agent): "Dear Spectators 2: A Bedtime
  Story" (titled "If a Tree")
Outlook Springs: "Dear Spectators," "We Are Taught," and
  "Imagine: A Love Song"

LIGATURES

for black bodies

This was a horrible event.

It should not happen again, and there already have been lessons learned and that is the positive side of this tragedy.

Already, steps have been taken to assure that these events do not reoccur:
• The city has bought body cams for all its officers. That will help
• Dash cams are on the way for CPD and suburban departments

—excerpt from the statement read by Prosecutor McGinty, as quoted in *Officers Will Not Be Charged in Tamir Rice Shooting Death* by DARCIE LORENO, JEN STEER, PEGGY GALLEK and ED GALLEK | *FOX8 Cleveland* | 1:02 PM, Dec. 28, 2015

Dear Spectators,

You will need a context for viewing—so
first, consider the noose, that birthmarked

ligature that brailled brown eyes use to scan images—
retinas fingerlike trace postcarded necks of bodies

born brown then noosed, born brown then picnic
blackened, born brown & then trophied

into ear or penis or vagina or tongue—
born brown & biologied into body

cam-ed bodies born brown then bulleted,
born brown then broken, born brown then bent—

born brown then esophagus-threaded through handcuff
born brown then bracketed by [hashtag & period].

Then period turns to question marked silhouette—her
2015 body, hangs—her standing kneel, bracketed by bars

looks so much like pause between prayer & dancing—
looks so much like a 1913 3 & ¼ by 5 cardboarded brown

body with soul smoking skyward, looks so much like *alive,
soaked in coal oil before being set on fire*—this reverse alchemy

a living brown body, all slick & shine then, dissolution—
a not-so mysterious transmuting, bone to blood to ash

  —& 2015 and '16 look so much like 1910—
See the silhouetted corpses of African Americans

[...]

shot from a 1920 Kodak, shot on a 1982 Sony, shot
on a 2015 dash cam, shot on a 2016 body cam.

—shot
      or dragged
           or tased
                or cuffed
                     or pounded against pavement—

these bodies born brown then catapulted into
lifeless silent film stars—surrounded by spectators.

The South Carolina police officer who shot and killed Walter Scott after he turned and ran says an infamous video does not show the whole story of what happened on the morning of April 4—and he says the truth will come out.

"Just that three seconds of the video came out. And everybody thought I was racist, and I just got out of my car and just shot him in the back for no reason," Officer Michael Slager told NBC News in a Skype interview from jail.

"That's what makes me upset is [sic] that nobody knows what actually happened," he said. "But now it's gonna come out."

The comments came as his lawyer outlined a defense: Slager didn't know Scott was unarmed, felt threatened, and made a quick decision to shoot because he believed Scott might pull a gun and shoot him first.

—excerpt from *Michael Slager, Cop Who Killed Walter Scott, Says He Felt Threatened* by CRAIG MELVIN | *NBC News* | 7:34 PM, Sept. 8, 2015

Next to Scott's Body:
An Officer's Confession

for Walter Scott

(His brake light out.)

    Him. Hands cuffed.

Me. Bent and bending. Dropping taser. I lie.

—he lies. Body down. Flesh pitted by five

of my service pistol's eight bullets.

    Difference is, I lie for a reason.

A white man, hand hugging gun hot as an open mouth, legs

running toward me is less—

   threatening than a black man running away—his

hands molded into batonless fists—torso folded

at waist, legs keeping pace like the last leg of a relay.

   C'mon. Say

you wouldn't be scared too.

In the McDonald case, Chicago officers were summoned by a 911 call to a neighborhood on the city's Southwest Side the night of Oct. 20, 2014, to investigate a report of a man with a knife trying to break into vehicles in a trucking yard. Officers came upon Mr. McDonald, who was holding a folding knife, and told him to drop it, Chicago officials have said. Mr. McDonald refused, the officers said, and he began walking or jogging away. Two officers followed him—one on foot, the other in a car—and called for backup, requesting that an officer carrying a Taser stun gun be sent to the area.

A police dashboard camera captured the end of the episode: Along a multilane commercial stretch of Pulaski Road, one of the six police officers at the scene fired his weapon, striking the teenager 16 times.

Some who have seen the video say that it shows the teenager, Laquan McDonald, being struck by a barrage of bullets, some hitting him even after he had fallen to the pavement. The teenager, who the authorities say was carrying a knife, was shot 16 times, according to a report from the Cook County medical examiner's office. Some of the bullets entered the back of his body.

—excerpt from *Video of Chicago Police Shooting a Teenager Is Ordered Released* by Monica Davey and Mitch Smith | *New York Times* | Nov. 19, 2015

13 Seconds on Pulaski:
Another Officer's Confession

for Laquan McDonald

(He punctured the tires of a car with his knife.)

And shit yeah, I'm scared
        of any black boy's moving—his
marking a deliberate line through my world—

so I set that body spinning
—a black top through thinning air—

     13 seconds
from start to
       motionless. He's holed and I'm—
the empty chamber—wholly intent on reloading.

A timeline of events after Eric Garner's death while he was being arrested on Staten Island:

Thursday, July 17, 2014: Eric Garner is arrested for allegedly selling untaxed cigarettes on Victory Boulevard and Bay Street in the Tompkinsville section of Staten Island. Cellphone video captures the unarmed 43-year-old black man being taken into custody, and he's heard saying "I can't breathe, I can't breathe" as officer Daniel Pantaleo places him in an apparent chokehold, a tactic prohibited by NYPD policy. Garner goes into cardiac arrest.

EMS workers arrive, and they do not appear to administer CPR on Garner. Garner is taken to Richmond University Medical Center, where he is pronounced dead.

—excerpt from video: *Man Dies During Arrest for Selling Illegal Cigarettes, NYPD Says* by NICHOLAS RIZZI and AIDAN GARDINER | *DNAinfo* | 7:58 AM, July 18, 2014

What I Learned at the Academy:
Another Officer's Confession

for Eric Garner

(He was illegally selling cigarettes.)

It was never supposed to be
a chokehold. Just a wrestling
move I learned at the Academy
so I locked one arm under his
slipped the other around his torso—

how else to let him know there is
no sense in resisting? His worded defense—
my hands getting tense—just let me tip
the perp, make him lose his balance.

Just let me ground him.

More choke than hold, my arm—
the sound of begging, his breath—
his head to concrete, my hand—

my right arm around his thick of neck.

About 12:45 a.m., said Moultrie, Victor left on a borrowed bike. From there to where the chase started was about 4 1/2 miles. But it was about 1:45 a.m. that Officer Jerald Ard spotted Victor. Where Victor went after leaving Moultrie's house is unclear.

Ard would later say that he tried to stop Victor because he had seen him at a construction site and thought he may have stolen something. But witness Victor Stallworth said he saw Victor ride his bicycle past the construction site without stopping. Months later, Ard gave investigators a different reason for stopping Victor: He didn't have a light on his bike — only two reflectors.

A video camera on the dashboard of Ard's squad car recorded the brief chase: Ard spotted Victor and did a fast U-turn to stop him. When Victor didn't stop, Ard veered to the wrong side of the street and up on the sidewalk behind the teenager.

The officer revved the motor, his tires screeching, as he followed Victor into the side yard of an apartment building. With his flashers and PA system on, Ard yelled at Victor to "stop the bike."

It is unclear why Victor disobeyed the order to stop, but the teenager continued pedaling, trying to escape. Ard followed his every move, driving in and out of the wrong lane of traffic and up onto the sidewalk again. One minute and seven seconds into the chase Ard fired his Taser at Victor, who made a turn into a parking lot. About two seconds later, Victor fell to the ground and Ard ran over him ...

The day after the funeral, Florida Department of Law Enforcement investigator Eli Lawson called Cassandra Steen's newly-hired attorney, Aaron Watson, and told him that TV news was about to report that a paramedic had found a gun in Victor's pocket.

A video, taken from the dashboard of another officer's car, recorded what happened in the minutes before the discovery: Three officers squatted next to Ard's car, looking under it at Victor. Ard unlocked the passenger side of his car and got something out. The object is light-colored and floppy, but isn't clearly visible. Ard, holding the object, crawled under the car next to Victor's body and stayed there for 40 seconds. Two minutes later, paramedics found a 9mm silver and black semiautomatic in Victor's pocket.

Lab tests showed the gun had been wiped clean. No fingerprints were on it—not Victor's, not anyone's.

—excerpt from *Death of Teen on Bike Shows Risks of Expanded Use of Tasers* by MEG LAUGHLIN | *Tampa Bay Times* | 2:25 PM, July 30, 2010

Click-Click:
An Officer's Confession

for Victor Steen

(... had seen him at a construction site and thought he may have stolen something. or *He didn't have a light on his bike—only two reflectors.)*

Something shapes him
into that smoke-slippery shadow I just saw
shift from construction site to concrete.
Not my fault he won't stop, I try
to bull-horn him to his feet—

Not sure if it is all my steel and four
wheels barreling after his two
that make his black body all limbed
motion—but I know it's the *click-click* split
from this hand through that Florida night—

sound all snake's rattle—
    shock that follows bite—
        that'll hurtle him from spin to flight—
           to motionless

—A chassied tree branch.
    A tangle of dogwood or willow—

He lies. I slide under, lie—
next to him. Look the length
of axle to oil pan, then glide
my hand into his pocket—
gift him steel and lead.

        Difference is—
I lie for a reason.

On Nov. 22, 2014, Tamir was playing outside the Cudell Recreation Center with an airsoft pellet gun when a bystander called 911 to report that a "guy" was pointing a gun at people. The caller noted that person might be a juvenile, and that the gun might be a toy. But a dispatcher did not pass along that information to Loehmann and Garmback, who responded to the call.

Most officers on the scene described Tamir as roughly 200 pounds, and said he appeared to be 18 to 20 years old. Officers also said the gun beside Tamir appeared real, even up close.

According to investigators, who reviewed surveillance camera footage of the shooting, Loehmann fired twice and struck Tamir once "within an approximate time frame of 1 to 2 seconds after Officer Loehmann exited the vehicle." Loehmann shot Tamir from 4.5 to 7 feet away before tripping backward and hurting his ankle.

Loehmann later told another police officer on the scene, "He [Tamir] gave me no choice, he reached for the gun and there was nothing I could do."

Three and a half minutes after arriving on the scene, the officers were calling for EMS and asking the rescue crew to "step it up" and get there quickly. Neither of the officers performed any immediate first aid on the wounded boy. Neither had any medical training to help a shooting victim, nor did they have any medical equipment in their police car.

An FBI agent trained as a paramedic heard about the shooting on a radio and headed to the scene. The agent, whose name is redacted in the report, told investigators he performed some basic first aid on Tamir, who was still alive and responsive though his wound exposed some intestines.

At one point, Tamir reached for the agent's hand. Provided only a pair of rubber gloves by Cleveland police, the agent cleared Tamir's airway and examined the wound while waiting several minutes for an ambulance crew to arrive.

An ambulance took Tamir to MetroHealth Medical Center, where he died early the next morning. The Cuyahoga County Medical Examiner's office ruled his death a homicide. An autopsy showed the bullet had perforated a major blood vessel and intestines, and fractured his pelvis.

—excerpt from *Tamir Rice Investigation Released: The Big Story* by IDA LIESZKOVSZKY | *Northeast Ohio Media Group* | 7:00 AM, June 14, 2015

We Are Taught:
Another Officer's Confession

for Tamir Rice

(A Black Male, camouflage hat, grey jacket, and black
sleeves at or near the swing set waving a gun and
pointing at people.)

See, we were *trained to keep eyes*
on hands—we were trained
that *hands may kill*—we
were trained to *tap-tap*

a hole as round as an open mouth—
trained to watch as nickel-tipped teeth
tear through a torso of grown flesh
to leave an openness all clean-edged

                           —and gaping

but we were not taught to decipher
a black boy's body from the bulk
of a black man. Were taught to fix
on the hands without reading for

wrinkle or smooth. We were taught
to look at the elbow, wait for when
it begins to pendulum toward our
ticking hearts. *We were taught to shoot*

and move. We were taught
that the *car is a coffin.*
We put his sister
there to wait.

Imagine: A Love Song

for and "from" Sandra Bland

Imagine I am not fingernail
       scrapings—imagine I
am not neck, or vagina or legs—
Imagine I am not a
knot.

Imagine you are not a toe tag.
Not rubber band that encircles
the right wrist. Not a black

hooded, zip-up sweatshirt (cut)
black—   Not black   with white
lettering, blue jeans, black—boxers
(cut), two black—   shoes
and two black—   socks.

Imagine you

      are not tags

attached to both great toes—ankles
tied together—a boy altered
by surgical intervention—Imagine
      you are not
a recovered bullet, metal jacketed
      moderately deformed,
      mushrooming
at the nose—"TR"

      inscribed on its base

[…]

Imagine? Instead?—

We—   are

                    not

kidney, or head, or hands. Imagine
we—are not unremarkable, not—
skin as thin or disposable or ordinary
as a plastic garbage bag.

Imagine us

not on display

not
          pathology

                              or pathologized

Imagine We—

backs, still vertical—still alive. Not

          twisted until
                              made lethal.

Dear Spectators 2:
A Bed Time Story

He is menacing she is angry he is big
she is screaming he is raping she is running
he is she is he is she is he is she is he is

they are—

black trees falling in a black forest—
cut down by the axed tongue of a nation's origin
that's more myth than story. If you want me to tuck
you in at bed time, I will tell you about Old Glory.

She was conceived by conjurers egged and spermed
by white whaled wanderers who wandered wayless
on seas so high they lost their way and called it
discovering. Then she was birthed fiber twisted

and fixed by hands so quick to thimble her, they left
her red and white and hovering—afterbirth fluttering
in wind so thin she was left mothering the blue-bruised
female, brown, and black bodies they'd begun fucking

since well before they got here. Well, before they got
here they'd already cracked open whole countries and
continents sharpened humans into soldiers sharpened
soldiers into armies sharpened armies into the teeth

of a mouth that gorged on their contents and still they
were not content, not full, not satiated. Fast forward
almost twelve-score and more years to: *He is raping she*
is angry he is big she is screaming he is running she is he is

[...]

she is he they all become headlines. From a Virginia
runaway advertisement to a current news story about
the background of another dead black body even before
their blood stops stippling pavement, black and brown

people's stories have been spun so quickly and so
thoroughly so that suddenly our lives seem to justify
the ending of them. Black and brown bodies have been
named from auctions blocks to blogs and back again as

those people for centuries; and that identity created
and written by people who would lynch, police officers
who would shoot to kill and judges and juries who would
acquit, has been fatal. This is not new. But some of you want

a child friendly bed time story, get comfortable, tuck in
and let them wrap up in Old Glory—then scroll down.
See a picture of a black boy or black girl, a black man
or a black woman, a black person or a black person

and you wonder is she or isn't she, is he or isn't he, are they or
aren't they and each isn't but each is, you wonder is it another
story of or isn't it? You wonder is it a graduation or is it the grave?
Are they another hashtag or are they the college graduate whose

college acceptance is like the exhale of a pitcher's save at the bottom
of the 9th. See you want to exhale, you'd rather exhale because digging
deep is not what you want to do right now. You'd rather slide finger
up screen like eraser across slate, scroll past the hate as if it's not

been sown into the fabric of your pillow, scroll past as if the weeping
willow wrapped around a brown neck isn't the dream catcher we always
wake to, scroll past the white police officer whose dream it is to catch
and rape her, scroll past as if this story isn't ours because it is—see we

have moved way beyond Old Glory to *He is raping she is angry he is*
big she is screaming he is running she is He is she is he is she is he is she is

He was 12
She was 37
He was 19
She was 34
He was 18
She was 47
He was 26
She was 16
He was 6
She was 22
He was 22
He was 19
She was 55
He was 12
She was 7
He was 23
She was 3
He was 17
She was 15
He was 13
She was human
He was human
She was breathing
He was breathing
She was
He was
She was
He was
She was
He was
She was
He was
They were.

ABOUT THE RATTLE CHAPBOOK PRIZE

The annual Rattle Chapbook Prize offers at least one winning chapbook $2,000 and free distribution to all of *Rattle*'s print subscribers. For more information, and to order other chapbooks from the series, visit:

www.rattle.com/chapbooks

2016 | Winner:
> *3arabi Song* by Zeina Hashem Beck

2016 | Runners-Up:
> *Kill the Dogs* by Heather Bell
> *Ligatures* by Denise Miller
> *Turn Left Before Morning* by April Salzano

Denise Miller is a professor, poet, and mixed media artist whose publications include poems in *Dunes Review*, *African American Review* and *Blackberry: A Magazine*. She was named the 2015 Willow Books Emerging Poet, an AROHO Waves Discussion Fellowship awardee, a finalist for the Barbara Deming Money for Women Fund, and a Hedgebrook Fellow. Her full-length book, *Core*, was released by Willow Books in November 2015 and has since been nominated for a 2016 American Book Award and a 2016 Pushcart Prize. Miller has also been named a 2016 William Randolph Hearst Fellow at the American Antiquarian Society. She lives in Kalamazoo, Michigan.

www.makedo.weebly.com

You will need a context for viewing—so
first, consider the noose, that birthmarked

ligature that brailled brown eyes use to scan images—
retinas fingerlike trace postcarded necks of bodies

born brown then noosed, born brown then picnic
blackened, born brown & then trophied

into ear or penis or vagina or tongue—
born brown & biologied into body

cam-ed bodies born brown then bulleted,
born brown then broken, born brown then bent—

born brown then esophagus-threaded through handcuff
born brown then bracketed by [hashtag & period].

ISBN 978-1-931307-32-1

POETRY / $6
Cover art: Bridget A. Saunders
www.Rattle.com

rattle